Men Who Throw Children Off Cliffs

(...and other things neurotic dads worry about)

Written by Steve Sessions & Pete Goldfinger

Illustrated by Steve Sessions

Riley has a
tummy ache!

Mommy thinks they should go to the doctor,
just to be safe.

Daddy remembers reading about some parents in Portland who took their little girl to a hospital for a tummy ache and she somehow ended up with sepsis!

Mommy tells Daddy to stop talking
because he's making everyone
nervous.

Besides, she says, it's probably just
a little bug.

Daddy says that's exactly what
those parents in Portland thought.

Daddy wonders if Mommy
really understands how
serious sepsis can be.

At the doctor's office, Daddy takes the
special medication he was prescribed last
time Riley wasn't feeling well.

While Riley is seen by the doctor,
Daddy gets in the fetal position to await
the bad news.

But on the plus side, his medication
makes him dream of unicorns!

It's a miracle!

The doctor says it was just a little bug and Riley will be better in no time!

The nice doctor even gives Riley a stuffed animal to take home.

Mommy decides that next time Riley has a
tummy ache, Daddy will just stay at home.

THE END

Riley gets
a pet!

Riley finds a mouse in the back yard and
Mommy says she can keep him!

Riley names her mouse Charlie and
makes him a home out of
an old shoe box.

But Daddy is worried. See, there's this thing
called Hantavirus Pulmonary Syndrome that
most people don't know about.

The next morning

Charlie is gone!

Daddy comforts Riley and tells her Charlie
is probably back with his family where he's
safe and happy...

THE END

Riley learns
to swim!

Daddy hires a guy named Thad
to teach Riley how to swim!

Daddy typically doesn't trust guys named Thad,
but he'll give him the benefit of the doubt.

Daddy notices Riley is struggling and
seems to be choking on water! But
know-it-all Thad
says this is how they learn.

That night,
Mommy kisses
Riley goodnight
and tells her
she's going to be
a great swimmer
one day!

Later that night, Daddy reads about something called secondary drowning...

Secondary drowning is what happens when kids drown hours after they are out of the water.

There are no symptoms!

Daddy is positive Riley has secondary drowning. After all, she has no symptoms.

So, Daddy wakes Riley every 15 minutes to
make sure she's still breathing. Mommy yells
at Daddy and reminds him that Riley has
school in the morning.

☐ Daddy politely reminds Mommy that Riley
won't have school tomorrow if she dies
from secondary drowning.

THE END

Riley goes to
the beach!

Riley goes to the beach for a **day of fun in the sun!**

She wants to dig in the sand for buried pirate treasures. Daddy thinks she's more likely to dig up a used syringe contaminated with Hepatitis C.

Riley decides to practice her swimming in the ocean.

Daddy takes a moment to imagine all the things that could get her if **she's not careful.**

Mommy tells Daddy to relax. But Mommy doesn't know the first thing about the dangers lurking in the ocean. For example, the Box Jellyfish...

These evil sea creatures attack in shallow water and inflict venom so poisonous that their victims are rendered unconscious from pain, yet somehow continue to scream in agony.

And then they die!

SEE!
Jellyfish are very painful
BREAKING NEW
INFORMATION · WORLD · BUSINESS · FINANCE · LIFESTYLE · TRAVEL · SPOR
BOX JELLYFISH
STRIKE AGAIN

Mommy and Riley decide to
leave the beach and go to a
movie instead.

THE END

Riley goes to
the carnival!

The carnival is in town

and Riley can't wait to go on all the rides.

Daddy wonders how many carnival workers are actually ex-convicts... He figures it's gotta be upwards of seventy percent.

Riley wants to go on the Ferris wheel!

Daddy tries to explain what can happen if you go
on a ride that's been assembled by
murderers and kidnappers...

NEWS
CHOPPER
4

CHURRO

We should have seen this coming!
It's okay if you want to remarry.
Great, now I'm permanently disabled.

Daddy feels as if, all in all,
this was a pretty successful day!

THE END

Riley scores
a goal!

Riley plays in her first soccer game.

Mommy and Daddy
cheer from the sideline!

Daddy wonders if anyone else notices the fat boy
who keeps knocking over the smaller kids?

Mommy informs Daddy he
can't call other kids fat.
Especially in public.

(This reminds Daddy of a story he read about the
municipalities using reclaimed water in public
parks, which some doctors think can cause cancer!
But that's a story for another day.)

Mommy tells Riley not to worry
and to have fun.

But Daddy knows that Riley's missed goal will result in **low self-esteem, an expensive drug habit, and a dead-end job.**

So in a sense, Daddy cares more about
Riley than Mommy does.

Riley finally scores a goal!

After the game, Daddy congratulates
her on a great shot!

Then he introduces himself to the stocky kid.

THE END

Riley's first
sleepover!

Mommy said

YES!

Anna's Daddy answers the door wearing cargo
shorts and smelling like a Foghat concert.

He assures Riley's parents that there's nothing to
worry about because he and his bros are going to
be home all night jamming in the basement.

Daddy promises Riley she can **definitely**
have a sleepover next year!

Maybe.

THE END

Riley's summer
vacation!

JUNE
13 14 15 16 17 18 19
20 21 22 23 24 25 26
27 28 29 30

Daddy has taken a whole month off work,
even though his boss made him
feel guilty about it.

... so there's a pretty good chance I'll be unemployed when we get back.
MAINE
3,271 MILES

Mommy rented a house on something called Airbnb
where you stay in someone else's house and
even use their sheets!

The listing said the home "has character,"
which Daddy believes is code for
"the roof might collapse!"

Daddy can't stop thinking about the thick, curly
hair he saw on the pillow

Daddy decides he should probably call a
cleaning crew.

That night Daddy realizes the house has
an even bigger problem.
Riley's bedroom faces the street!

Daddy tells Mommy this is basically giving meth
addicts an invitation to kidnap Riley.

Mommy tells Daddy he can't talk like that in front of Riley because it frightens her.

Daddy says if Riley is frightened now, imagine how
she'll feel when the meth addicts have her!

THE END

Riley goes
on a hike!

Mommy and Daddy take Riley on a hike.
Riley runs down the trail to a rocky point
overlooking the ocean.

The boats look so tiny from up here.

Daddy notices a man sitting by himself,
reading a book.

The man is wearing dress shoes with shorts,
which Daddy thinks is
borderline psychotic behavior!

Daddy tells Mommy they should leave because
this type of weirdo is obviously one of those
men who throw children off cliffs!
He probably waits around all day for kids to
get too close to the edge...

Mommy says Daddy is being ridiculous.
But Daddy knows **evil does exist** in the
world, even if Mommy refuses to see it.

Mommy tells Daddy if he doesn't go back to
therapy soon, he'll have to go live at
Uncle Stan's house for a while.

It wouldn't be the first time.

THE END

ABOUT THE AUTHORS

Steven Sessions & Pete Goldfinger met through their incredible wives and bonded immediately over their love/hatred of golf, parties, writing, people and life in Los Angeles. That bond was further strengthened when they each became fathers of daughters. Though they are film and tv writers by trade, they were compelled to write this book because nobody would listen to them. They hope it will provide an unfiltered look into the dark recesses of their addled minds and find its way into your heart.

www.ingramcontent.com/pod-product-compliance
Lightning Source LLC
Chambersburg PA
CBHW040522120726
48010CB00006B/207